MAGIC MONSTERS
Act the Alphabet

by Jane Belk Moncure
illustrated by Helen Endres

THE CHILD'S WORLD

ELGIN, ILLINOIS 60120

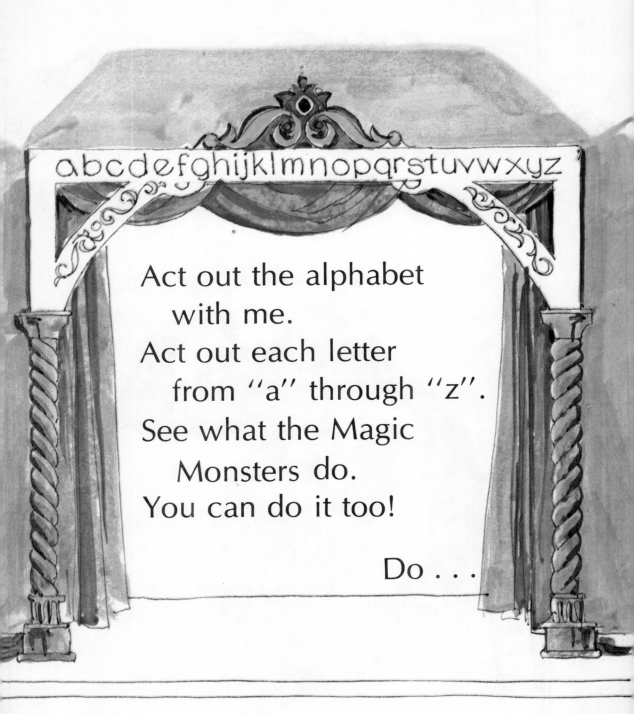

abcdefghijklmnopqrstuvwxyz

Act out the alphabet
   with me.
Act out each letter
   from "a" through "z".
See what the Magic
   Monsters do.
You can do it too!

Do . . .

Aa

acrobatics with
an
ape.

Bb

Blow
bubbles with a
baboon.

Cc

Clown with a creepy crocodile.

Dd Dance with a dragon from the deep lagoon.

Ee

Eat with an
elephant,
even though
it's green.

Make a . . .

Ff

funny
face at
Frankenstein
on Halloween.

Gg

Gobble with a
goblin.
Giggle with a
ghost.

Hop around a haunted house, but do not scare your host.

l i

Ice skate
with a
snowman.

Jump rope
with a
bear.

Kk

Kiss a
kitty as she
rides a broomstick
in the air.

Laugh at a long-legged monster. Sit upon its lap.

Mm

Make
music with a
mummy . . .

but . . .

never
nod or
nap.

Open the door
for an
ogre.

Play his
piccolo.

If he starts to

quarrel,
you had
better go.

R r

Ride a
rocket with a
robot and a . . .

skeleton or two,
and a very
scary
scarecrow.
What a very
scary crew!
        You . . .

S s

T t

turn and
twist and
tumble,
topsy-turvy,

upside down . . .

before you land quite safely
in a Magic Monster town.

Then you . . .

visit with a
vampire on a
very scary night.

And a . . .

Ww

witch flies in
to play
with you.

(Do not turn off the light!)

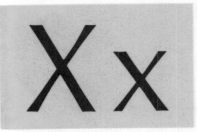

X marks the
spot where a
shadow appears.

Yackety-
yak, a . . .

zombie
appears,

to . . .

abcdefghijklmnopqrstuvwxyz

zip up the curtain
at the end of the act,
the Magic Monsters'
alphabet act.